# We Worship Here

# MUSLIM MOSQUE

Angela Wood & Emma Trithart

W

FRANKLIN WATTS

LONDON • SYDNEY

Franklin Watts

First published in paperback
in Great Britain in 2022 by
The Watts Publishing Group

Credits
Series Editor: Sarah Peutrill
Series Designer: Anthony Hannant,
Little Red Ant

Consultant and content editor:
Shaykh Ibrahim Mogra, The Muslim
Council of Britain, Mogra Faith &
Culture Consultancy

ISBN 978 1 4451 6174 7

Printed in Dubai

Franklin Watts
An imprint of
Hachette Children's Group
Part of The Watts Publishing Group
Carmelite House
50 Victoria Embankment
London EC4Y 0DZ

An Hachette UK Company

www.hachette.co.uk
www.hachettechildrens.co.uk

# CONTENTS

Words in **bold** are in the glossary on page 28.

# Mosques Around the World

**Mosques** are places where Muslims pray to God and meet to study. The **Arabic** name for mosque is masjid. Muslims also pray at home.

*There are mosques all over the world.*

*There are no pictures or statues of **Allah** or the **Prophet** Muhammad (peace be upon him) inside a mosque. Instead the walls and ceilings are decorated with beautiful patterns.*

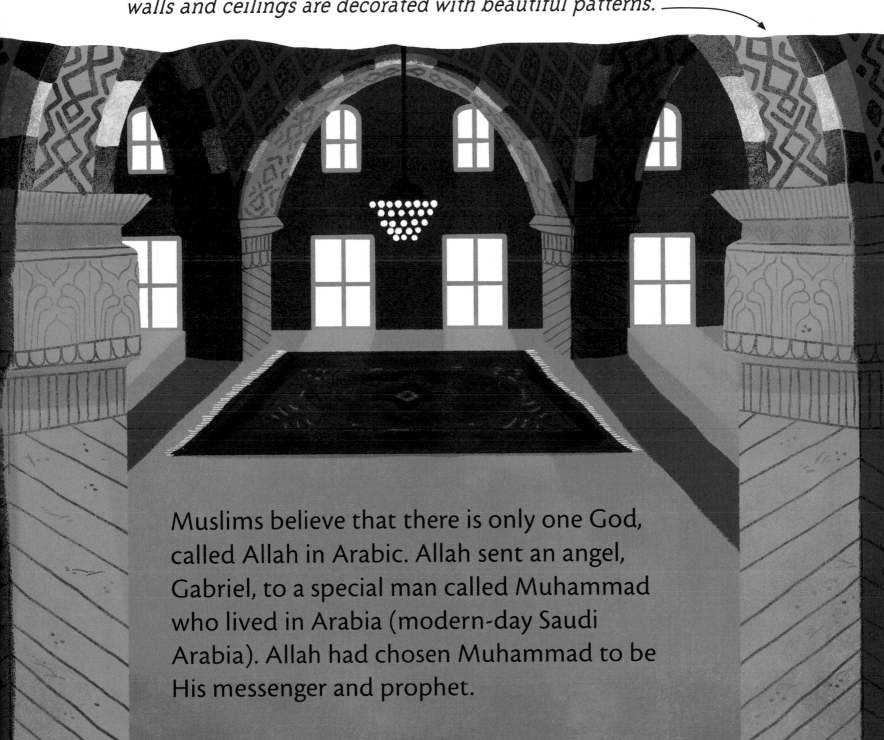

Muslims believe that there is only one God, called Allah in Arabic. Allah sent an angel, Gabriel, to a special man called Muhammad who lived in Arabia (modern-day Saudi Arabia). Allah had chosen Muhammad to be His messenger and prophet.

# PRAYER TIMES

Muslims can go to the mosque
at any time but midday on
Friday is especially important.
Muslims pray five times a day.
The exact times of some of the
prayers change according to
sunrise and sunset times.

*Mosques have clock boards
showing the prayer times
for each day. The clocks
start at the top on the right.
The dark clock shows the
time for the prayers at
midday on Friday.*

*Many now have electronic
boards to display the prayer
times and other activities.*

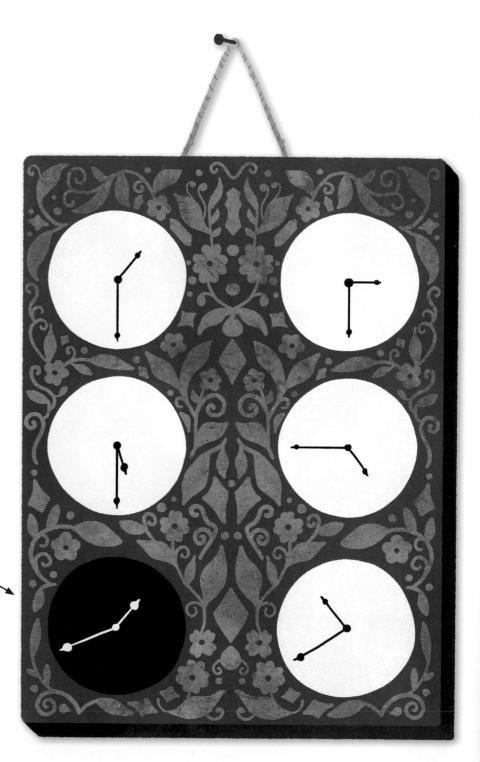

8

# THE CALL TO PRAYER

When it is time to pray a **mu'adhdhin** calls out the adhan (call to prayer) from a loudspeaker.

*This is a mu'adhdhin calling people to prayer. In some countries the call is broadcast on the television and radio.*

# THE KA'BAH

Muslims always face a particular direction in prayer, called the **Qiblah**. This is in the direction of a building called the **Ka'bah**, which is in the city of **Makkah** in Saudi Arabia. The very first prayer made to Allah was at the Ka'bah.

The Prophet Muhammad lived in Makkah and taught people the important messages he had from Allah.

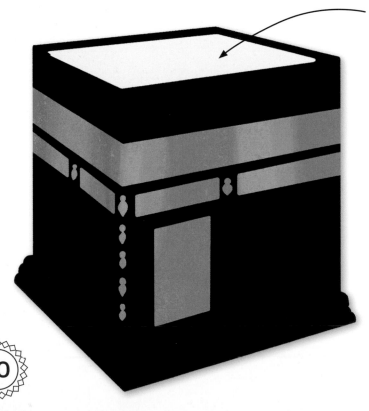

*This is a model of the cube-shaped Ka'bah.*

Muslims try to visit Makkah
at least once in their life.
This special visit is called Hajj.

# INSIDE A MOSQUE

The main part of a mosque is the prayer hall. There is no furniture in the hall but there are carpets or mats to pray on. Men and women wash in separate rooms and also pray separately.

*Here Muslim men are praying close together. The carpets help them to stay in straight lines.*

13

# THE QUR'AN

Inside every mosque are copies of the Qur'an. The Qur'an is the special book for Muslims. It is written in Arabic and contains the messages that Allah sent to the Prophet Muhammad. It is treated with love and **respect**.

*The Qur'an is placed on a stand to keep it clean and to show how important it is.*

Muslims try to learn some or all of the Qur'an by heart in Arabic and learn its meaning.

# The Mihrab and Minbar

Every mosque has a place on one wall, called a **mihrab**. This shows the direction of prayer (Qiblah). Near the mihrab there is a platform called a **minbar**. This is where the imam, or prayer leader, stands every Friday at midday when he speaks to the people.

*This is a minbar on its own.*

A mihrab

Here the mihrab and minbar are together in the mosque. The imam is standing on the minbar facing the people.

# GETTING READY TO PRAY

When Muslims go into a mosque, they take off their shoes. This is to show their respect and also to keep the mosque clean. Then they wash carefully. The washing, is called **wudu'**.

It is important to be very clean to pray to Allah. There is an order for washing.

*1. First Muslims wash their hands.*

*2. Then they wash their mouth, nose and whole face.*

3. Then they wash their arms including elbows.

4. Next they pass wet hands over their head, inside their ears and across the back of their neck.

5. Lastly they wash their feet, including the ankles and scrub between their toes, with their little finger.

# PRAYER POSITIONS

Muslims pray with their whole bodies. They use different positions in prayer, a number of times. They stand, bow and put their head on the ground. All the three positions together are called a **rak'ah**.

*The three positions are shown here.*

By bending and bowing until their forehead is on the ground, Muslims show how great Allah is. At the same time, they say 'Allahu Akbar' which means 'Allah is the Greatest'.

# MUSLIM DRESS

It is important for Muslims to dress in a way that shows their respect for Allah and others.

Some Muslim girls and many Muslim women keep their heads covered at all times. Here a group of Muslim girls are praying together.

# Helping Others

Many mosques have a collection box. Muslims believe that they should help other people as much as they can. One way they do this is to give money to charity. This is called **sadaqah**. Doing good things is sadaqah too.

Once a year all adult Muslims give a **percentage** (2.5%) of their wealth to help poor people. This is called **zakah**.

This girl is putting money in the collection box at the mosque.

25

# A School in a Mosque

All mosques have classes for children during the week after school or at weekends. In Arabic this school is called a madrasah. The children are taught how to lead a Muslim way of life. They also read the Qur'an and some try to learn it by heart.

When they are young, boys and girls study together. When they are older, they have separate classes.

Here a group of children are learning Arabic.

# GLOSSARY

**Allah** the Arabic name for God

**Arabic** the language spoken in Saudi Arabia and other countries in the Middle East and North Africa

**imam** the person who leads the prayers in the mosque

**Ka'bah** the cube-shaped building in Makkah. Muslims pray in the direction of the Ka'bah

**Makkah** the city in Saudi Arabia where the Prophet Muhammad was born. Muslims try to go to Makkah at least once in their lives

**mihrab** a place on the wall of the prayer hall that shows the direction for prayer

**minbar** a short staircase with a platform on top where the imam stands to speak to the people

**mosque** the place where Muslims meet to pray and study together

**mu'adhdhin** the person who calls Muslims to prayer. (It is also written as muezzin.)

**percentage** (also written as %) an amount in each 100, so 2.5% means 2.5 (two and a half) out of 100

**prophet** a messenger for God. Muhammad is the Prophet of Allah

**Qiblah** the direction of prayer

**Qu'ran** the Muslim holy book

**rak'ah** a set of positions for prayer

**respect** to treat well

**sadaqah** charity

**wudu'** washing before prayer

**zakah** giving money to poor people once a year

# INDEX